EDITED BY

a green thought in a green shade

poetry in the garden

THE POETRY SOCIETY

First published in 2000
by the Poetry Society

Design/layout by Stephen Troussé
at the Poetry Society

Jacket photo by Gina Glover

Printed by Grillford Ltd, 26 Peverel Drive, Granby,
Bletchley, Milton Keynes MK1 1QZ

ISBN 1 900771 26 8

Contents

Poetry Places

In 1997 the Poetry Society received a substantial grant from the 'Arts for Everyone' budget of the Arts Council of England Lottery Department to put into effect an innovative scheme to bring poetry to new audiences. This two-year programme of residencies, placements and projects aimed to explore the unique role that poetry can play in different settings. More than 130 poets have been involved in a variety of projects, ranging from forests, fish and chip shops and festivals to galleries, museums, parks and even an off-shore gas platform.

Poets have worked with drug users, sex offenders, lawyers, executives, teachers, teenagers, children and workers of all kinds as well as with poetry enthusiasts around the country. They have also worked – arguably a more traditional, more gentle association – in a number of gardens. At Chelsea Physic Garden, Sarah Maguire 'planted' poems amongst the flowers. At Heale Gardens, Alice Oswald wrote a poem based on a Japanese Noh play, which was recorded and placed at the bottom of a well. Eleanor Cooke explored the magic of the Botanical Garden in Birmingham with local children of all ages, while at Glasgow's Botanic Gardens Gerry Loose organised a medley of events, including a May Day parade and a Valentine tree, reflecting the diversity both of the local population and of the garden itself. Their essays, together with contributions from arts producer Theresa Bergne and Chelsea Physic Garden Education Officer Dawn Sanders, give a sense of the rich possibilities for poetry in the garden.

Christina Patterson,
Director, Poetry Society
May 2000

SARAH MAGUIRE

Introduction: a green thought in a green shade

In the beginning was a garden. And a poet to write about the garden. The garden, and the plants it nurtures, is a subject which has occupied poets of all times and places more consistently than any other apart from love and its inconsistencies. Think then of the bewildering possibilities facing a poet let loose in a garden…

Poems and gardens are inextricably intertwined. Even the language, the original words used for both, stems from the same roots (and even the language I use to describe this connection is inescapably metaphorically botanic). Take the entry for the word 'Posy' in the *OED*:

> *Now arch. Or dial. 1533. (Syncopated f. POESY.) 1. A short motto, orig. a line or verse of poetry, inscribed on a knife, within a ring, as a heraldic motto, etc. 2. A bunch of flowers; a nosegay, a bouquet. Now somewhat arch. or rustic. 1573. b. A collection of 'flowers' of poetry or rhetoric. Cf. ANTHOLOGY. arch. 1569.*

And one of the examples quoted by the *OED* for this entry is the following couplet by Christopher Marlowe: 'I will make thee beds of roses, / And a thousand fragrant posies'.

The first entry we find for 'Poesy' unsurprisingly reads: '= POETRY'. Then turning to 'Anthology', we learn that the term comes to us from 'anther', the Greek word for flower (now of course used in [botanical] English to refer to the part of the flower which stores pollen). The *OED* definitions of anthology are part literary, part botanical: 'a collection of the flowers of verse, ie small choice poems, esp. epigrams; orig. applied to the Gr. collections so called'; and, 'a treatise on flowers'.

But what of gardens themselves? Well, the originating idea of paradise in the Jewish, Christian and Muslim traditions is the Garden of Eden. Indeed, 'paradise' itself comes from a Greek word first used by Xenophon to describe the pleasure-gardens of the Persian kings. It's from the East, from ancient Mesopotamia, that the idea of the garden as a place of recreation and delight, rather than a space to grow useful plants, comes to us. And these eastern gardens are celebrated in some of the most ancient poetry, that written in Sumerian, the language of Babylonia, over 4,000 years ago; in *The Epic of Gilgamesh*, the king himself sings praises of a city graced with gardens and orchards. Some of the oldest known poetry written by women, in ancient Egypt between 1567 and 1085 BC, uses the language of flowers and the site of a garden to speak the language of love:

> So small are the flowers of Seamu
> Whoever looks at them feels like a giant.

> I am the first among your loves,
> Like a freshly sprinkled garden of grass and perfumed flowers.

> Pleasant is the channel you have dug
> In the freshness of the north wind.[1]

For those of us in the West, the original, and originating, garden comes to us in the language of *The King James Bible*, specifically in two entries. The first, of course, is 'Genesis' 2: 8-10

> And the Lord God planted a garden eastward in Eden; and there he put the man whom he had formed.
> And out of the ground made the Lord God to grow every tree that is pleasant to the sight, and good for food; the tree of life also in the middle of the garden, and the tree of knowledge of good and evil.
> And a river went out of Eden to water the garden; and from thence it was parted, and became into four heads.

The second is this wonderfully sensual passage from 'The

Song of Solomon' 4:12-16

A garden inclosed is my sister, my spouse; a spring shut up, a fountain sealed.

Thy plants are an orchard of pomegranates, with pleasant fruits; camphire, with spikenard,

Spikenard and saffron; calamus and cinnamon, with all trees of frankincense: myrrh and aloes, with all the chief spices:

A fountain of gardens, a well of living waters, and streams from Lebanon.

Awake, O north wind; and come, thou south; blow upon my garden, that the spices thereof may flow out. Let my beloved come into his garden, and eat his pleasant fruits.

Poets, then, have been making stories set in gardens and making love with the language of flowers for as long as we can tell. But gardens have changed – and plants have changed – which means that, unsurprisingly, poems about plants and gardens have changed too, and not least because poetry in turn has altered radically over the centuries as well.

When I began to look for poems written about plants and gardens, I assumed that there'd be lots of examples to be found the further back I searched. In fact, the opposite seems to be the case: the real explosion in poems with a botanical theme took place in the twentieth century, with a notable efflorescence and change of direction during the Romantic period. The reasons for this are embedded in literary and social history, but I'll try and sketch out some of these changes, using some examples of poems about flowers. Gardens are another thing altogether, and for an introduction to the history of poems about gardens, I'd refer you to John Dixon-Hunt's *The Oxford Book of Garden Verse*.[2]

One of the oldest English poems with a flower in the title is 'Of a Rose, a Lovely Rose', written around 1400. But the rose is not quite the horticultural object we might expect these days, as the opening stanzas make clear:

OF A ROSE, A LOVELY ROSE
Of a Rose, a lovely Rose,
Of a Rose is all my song.

Listen, nobles old and young,
How this rose at outset sprung;
In all this world I know of none
I so desire as that fair rose.
    Of a Rose, etc.

The angel came from heaven's tower
To honour Mary in her bower,

And said that she should bare the flower

To break the Devil's chain of woes.

    Of a Rose, etc.

In Bethlehem that flower was seen,

A lovely blossom bright of sheen.

The rose is Mary, heaven's Queen;

Out of her womb that blossom rose.

    Of a Rose, etc.[3]

Rather than being an object commonly afflicted with black spot, this 'rose is Mary, heaven's Queen'. In other words, the rose in this poem is a symbol for the Virgin Mary, a common trope during the period. Divinely ordained, objects in the natural world were there to instruct and delight human beings in the ways of God. The interest of the poet was not with the rose as a flower, but in how it could be used as a symbol to enrich perceptions of the Virgin Mary and aid in her devotion.

Perhaps the most admired poem written about a flower in English is 'The Flower' by George Herbert (1593-1633):

THE FLOWER

How fresh, O Lord, how sweet and clean

Are thy returns! even as the flowers in spring,

To which, besides their own demean,
The late-past frosts tributes of pleasure bring.
        Grief melts away
        Like snow in May,
    As if there were no such cold thing.

    Who would have thought my shriveled heart
Could have recovered greenness? It was gone
        Quite underground; as flowers depart
To see their mother-root, when they have blown,
        Where they together
        All the hard weather,
    Dead to the world, keep house unknown.

    These are thy wonders, Lord of power,
Killing and quickening, bringing down to hell
        And up to heaven in an hour;
Making a chiming of a passing-bell.
        We say amiss
        This or that is:
    Thy word is all, if we could spell.

    Oh that I once past changing were,
Fast in thy Paradise, where no flower can wither!

Many a spring I shoot up fair,
Offering at heaven, growing and groaning thither;
Nor doth my flower
Want a spring shower,
My sins and I joining together.

But while I grow in a straight line,
Still upwards bent, as if heaven were mine own,
Thy anger comes, and I decline:
What frost to that? what pole is not the zone
Where all things burn,
When thou dost turn,
And the least frown of thine is shown?

And now in age I bud again,
After so many deaths I live and write:
I once more smell the dew and rain,
And relish versing. Oh, my only light,
It cannot be
That I am he
On whom thy tempests fell all night.

These are thy wonders, Lord of love,
To make us see we are but flowers that glide,

Which when we once can find and prove,

Thou hast a garden for us where to bide;

Who would be more,

Swelling through store,

Forfeit thy Paradise by their pride.

As in 'Of a Rose', Herbert is not interested in the botanical object of the flower – even to the extent of not specifying which particular flower he's concerned with – but rather how he can use it to illustrate his theme of spiritual decline and renewal. This is a common approach in poems written before the Romantics; pre-Romantic poets are overwhelmingly interested in using objects in the natural world as reflections on metaphysical problems, such as John Donne's famous metaphor of a pair of compasses in 'A Valediction: Forbidding Mourning' representing separated lovers. And, given that poems themselves work through their use of metaphor, we can hardly be surprised when a poem 'about' a flower turns out to be 'about' spiritual development. But while Herbert's poem may be something of a disappointment to a twenty-first century botanist, it is a remarkably moving example of a poet examining the eternal problems of loss and redemption though the medium of the growth of spring flowers. The strength of the poem lies in Herbert's decision not to specify which particular flower he's writing about: his concern is with the metaphysics of growth itself, and with the reparative power of love that makes redemption possible.

Compare Roethke's 'Carnations' with Michael Longley's very different sequence, 'Botany':

BOTANY

Duckweed

Afloat on their reflection, these leaves
With roots that reach only part of the way,
Will fall asleep at the end of summer,
Draw in their skirts and sink to the bottom.

Foxglove

Though the corolla dangles upside down,
Nothing ever falls out, neither nectar
Nor loosening pollen grains: a thimble,
Stall for the little finger and the bee.

Dock

Its green flowers attract only the wind
But a red vein may irrigate the leaf
And blossom into a blush or birthmark
Or a remedy for the nettle's sting.

Orchid

The tuber absorbs summer and winter,
Its own ugly shape, twisted arms and legs,
A recollection of the heat, one artery
Sprouting upwards to support a flower.[4]

Michael Longley (born in 1939) is a passionate botanist, and these are poems written so clearly with a botanist's precision and delicate powers of observation. Just like a botanist, Longley has dissected the plants. And, just like Herbert, Longley is not simply writing about the particular plants he describes; he too is concerned with mortality, with the possibilities of a second spring and, above all, with the dynamics of gender and sex. These botanically 'objective' poems are nothing of the sort. And in writing from this perspective, Longley very cleverly carries out a sleight of hand which indicates the impossibility of any so-called objective scientific language, especially the discourse of botany which is profoundly imbricated in notions of gender and which can never really be considered neutral in such debates.

Over the centuries, poets have turned to flowers and plants (and gardens) as a way of examining, observing and illuminating the world they inhabit. The manner in which they've approached their subject matter has depended upon the time they're writing – the literary and social conventions available to them – and the effects they've wanted to achieve. Flowers are both in the world and symbolic of the great subjects of lyric poetry: mortality and the possibility of love. Which is why poets will keep on writing poems about plants and flowers in many differing, memorable and surprising ways.

It's hardly surprising that poets given the scope of working in gardens, as they have done here under the auspices of the Poetry Places scheme, will respond to their brief in similarly differing and memorable ways, eager to exploit the rich potential of the garden as a poetic resource.

1: Anonymous: *Love Poems of Ancient Egypt*, translated by Ezra Pound and Noel Stock; reprinted in *The Penguin Book of Women Poets*, edited by Carol Cosman, Joan Keefe and Kathleen Weaver (Penguin:; Harmondsworth, 1979) p. 37.
2: Oxford University Press, 1994.
3: From *Medieval English Verse*, translated by Brian Stone (Penguin, revised edition 1971) pp.29-30.
4: From *The Echo Gate: Poems 1975-79* (London: Secker & Warburg, 1979).

SARAH MAGUIRE

Cross-fertilisation: poetry at Chelsea physic garden

The aim of this small project was to stimulate the connections between poetry and gardens; to interest horticulturists in poems about plants, and to inspire poets and poetry-readers to look at plants afresh. Given twelve days work at Chelsea Physic Garden, the easy option would have been to hold a series of creative writing workshops with staff or members of the public and leave. But Dawn Sanders, the inspirational and hard-working Education Officer at Chelsea, and I decided that we wanted to make a more permanent poetic mark on the gardens, one that could be an important resource long after the funding for this project had expired.

Chelsea Physic Garden was founded in 1673 by the Worshipful Society of the Apothecaries of London. At that time, botany and medicine were indistinguishable and the purpose of the garden was to allow medical students to study plants used in healing. Hence its title of 'physic' garden, the old name for the art of healing. As the study of plants became separated from medicine, newer 'botanic' gardens (most famously at Kew) were established. Chelsea is the only garden to retain not simply its original title but its original purpose: many of the plants grown there are used for scientific and medical research.

Chelsea is a small garden – three-and-a-half acres (two hectares) – close to the Chelsea Embankment, which is one of the appealing aspects of working there as the poet in residence. Not only is it possible to get a grasp of the gardens, but I've got to know the curator and the head gardener, as well as many of the staff who work there. Chelsea also has a history of working with artists, and has a fresh and flexible approach to interpretation.

Because Chelsea is a physic garden, it's laid out in a different way to other botanic gardens. Although Kew, for example, is the world's most important site for botanical research, most visitors to the garden are struck by the aesthetically designed planting schemes. Chelsea, on the other hand, whilst undeniably 'beautiful' is unusual in that the visitor is always conscious this is a 'working' garden; that the plants are there not for pleasure (simply) but for their function. This 'utilitarian' aspect of the garden of course allows for unexpected and pleasing juxtapositions of plants. The part of the garden where its scientific role most clearly takes precedence is in the Dicotyledonous Order Beds. It's here that we've decided to intervene with a little poetic ordering of our own.

The name 'dicotyledonous' means 'two seed-leaves'. All plants are either monocotyledons (with one seed-leaf: bulbs and grasses are the most common example) or dicotyledons (the far larger group, encompassing everything from rambling roses to the Giant Redwood Tree). Within these two main groups, plants can further be divided into family groups, here represented in the order beds. All botanic gardens will have order beds (the ones in Kew are quietly tucked away) because it's in the order beds that their function of being botanical rather than pleasure gardens is most clearly revealed. The order beds are the *raison d'être* of a botanic garden. The science of botany depends on classification, classification which most famously began in the eighteenth century with Linnaeus. He began collating plants into groups depending on their shared characteristics, such as the number of petals in their flowers and the arrangement of their reproductive systems (inflammatory stuff *circa* 1750). The system currently used in the order beds at Chelsea (and elsewhere) was further modified by the nineteenth-century botanists, George Bentham and Joseph Hooker. But these classification systems, whilst fascinating for botanists, can seem terribly off-putting to the casual visitor to the garden because the family resemblances simply can't be 'seen' by the untrained eye. There's no doubt that the order beds are the least examined part of Chelsea Physic Garden; all the more reason for our intervention there.

What we've decided to do is to 'plant' poems in the order beds, poems which, in some way, are connected to the plants. Gardens, of course, are full of plants which poets have written about. But the order beds are full of plants which very few poets will have heard about, let alone been inspired by into verse. There are forty-nine order beds at Chelsea, and my first (exhaustive) task was to 'map' the beds, noting down the names of plants which may have a matching poem (sunflower, anemone, peony etc.) or looking up the translation of the scientific name of the plant which could provide a clue ('Aster' means 'star' in Latin, for example).

Stage two was to track down suitable texts for the plants, a task which involved a certain amount of lateral thinking, given the raw material of the plants themselves. Let me give you some examples. The plant Valerian is strongly associated with sleep, indeed many people have taken Valerian for insomnia. I was particularly keen to include the work of certain poets in the scheme, notably Wilfred Owen, who visited Chelsea Physic Garden during his last visit to London before he went back to the trenches and met his death; and John Keats, who studied the plants at Chelsea as part of his training as a doctor. The Valerian plant was a wonderful opportunity as I remembered Owen's wonderful poem 'Asleep', written during the War, which begins as follows:

Under his helmet, up against his pack,

After the many days of work and waking,
Sleep took him by the brow and laid him back.

I managed to find three other places for Owen. One in the bed belonging to the plant family Rubiaceae, which means 'red', and which reminded me of his poem, 'Greater Love', and the lines: 'Red lips are not so red / And the stained stones kissed by the English dead'. The second linked to Campanula ('bell'): 'What passing bells for those that die as cattle?' from 'Anthem for Doomed Youth'. And the third with Pullmoniaria ('lungs') and the horrific 'froth-corrupted lungs' in 'Dulce et Decorum Est'. Keats found two homes: the first via Aster ('star') and his glorious last sonnet, 'Bright star, would I were stedfast as thou art'; and the second for the plant family Dipsaceae, linked to drink, which recalled these lines from 'Ode to a Nightingale':

O, for a draught of vintage! that hath been
Cool'd a long age in the deep-delved earth
Tasting of Flora and the country green,
Dance, and Provencal song, and sunburnt mirth!

Some plants of course were familiar and fortunate enough to have been celebrated in verse by great poets. William Blake lines now grace two of the beds. The Helianthus (sunflower) of course demands his 'Ah! Sunflower, weary of time'. And what else could you put next to a rose but 'O Rose, thou art sick' (even though the poor plant itself looks to be doing rather well)?

The final stage of planting the poems was to select a couple of lines from each poem, have them engraved on a standard plant label, and then 'plant' them amongst the blooms. We started with sixteen labels (time and money mean that more will have to wait) and Dawn Sanders and I had the enormous pleasure of planting them in the beds one afternoon in July. What's so lovely about the labels is how unobtrusive they are, how much they seem to be part of the garden already, how 'right' they feel – and the subtle impact they have on the order of things. There were some particularly felicitous couplings, my favourite being lines from John Clare's 'Hedgehog' poem (placed next to the spiny Echinops): 'The hedgehog hides beneath the rotten hedge / And makes a great round nest of grass and sedge'. The label itself, like the hedgehog, is tucked beneath the tall herbaceous plant amongst the leafmould.

I'm thrilled with the results – and so is Dawn – and we're both excited by the possibilities of taking the project further, both with labelling more plants and using them as tools for inspiration and instruction. I'm so delighted that Keats and Owen and Blake and Clare, as well as countless other poets old and new, have found a new home, a new poetic paradise to inhabit and to name.

DAWN SANDERS

The naming of plants

When you place your hands in the soil of an historical garden you are immersing yourself in an organic archeology made up of the cycle of planting, growing, cropping and decomposition. The pieces of china and old plant labels you find in the soil, along with the ancient tools in the potting shed, all have a history and that history has a particular language:

> Today we have naming of parts. Japonica
> glistens like coral in all of the neighbouring gardens,
> And today we have naming of parts.
>
> (Henry Reed, 'Naming of Parts')

In using Latin as its language the science of taxonomy precludes many mortals from understanding the naming and ordering of plants:

On the banks of the Euphrates find a secret garden cunningly walled.

There is an entrance, but the entrance is guarded. There is no way in for you... It may be some other day, that you will open a gate by chance, and find yourself again on the other side of the wall.

(Winterson, 1985)

For horticulturalists and scientists the ordering and naming of plants has woven a complex and tangled web through botanical gardens; even now they are debating whether to display the old systems of classification or to adopt the new.

This process of naming and ordering coupled with the low visitor circulation at the order beds seemed to create a natural starting point for planting poems in the garden: I was interested in the idea of poems becoming lost jewels in the undergrowth so that when visitors found them they came as surprises rather than known events. Both Sarah and I wanted to use poetry to intersect with, and subvert, traditional practices. From the order beds Sarah took names, essences of meaning, details of physiology and found poetic analogy.

Gardens are steeped in traditional practices and one of the customary procedures used by gardeners here, in the physic garden, is to mark newly planted seeds with coarse sand. We hope to write poems in this sand to create an ethereal piece of expression, with the potential of exposure to heavy rain, so that it might dissipate into the soil; providing a visual metaphor for the vulnerability of life itself.

I see gardens as very much a place of communication and debate. They are not just about history, they are not static places, they are dynamic. Language is an essential part of that dynamism. The garden writer Mary Keen once wrote that gardeners are silent poets; by inviting Sarah to sow the seeds of poetry in the physic garden we hope to give gardens another dimension; as a place of words: spoken, gestured, heard and seen.

WHY A POET IN THE GARDEN?

To make a journey through a garden is to become as the American writer Annie Dillard wrote 'a tissue of senses'. Gardens are sensual places and poetry can celebrate that sensuality:

His door leaned open to the flies,
And May, like tendrils, wandered in.
The earth rose gently to his knees:
The clouds moved closer than his skin.

Sun against ear, he heard the slight
Stamen and pistil touch for days,
Felt pollen cast aslant like light
Into the shadows of his eyes,

(Extract from 'Elegy for Simon Corl' by Botanist David Wagoner)

Gardens are also environments where cultures collide: death and decay, nurture and destruction, nature and wilderness, control and freedom, loss and manipulation. The process of constructing a botanical garden is not an apolitical one: indeed, Chelsea contains several historical icons of botanical imperialism. Firstly a replica of the travelling miniature greenhouse, the Wardian case, invented by Nathaniel Bagshaw Ward in Victorian times, which proved invaluable for the transportation of tea, coffee, rubber and quinine: key economic plants that changed the face of the world. Secondly Chelsea supplied Georgia cotton plantations with their first seeds to support an industry built on slave labour. Ruth Padel's poem 'Rosa Silvestris Russica' encapsulates the dualities of gardener, explorer and sometime thief:

How else should a scientist work
but join the politicians' raids on other worlds?
Afterwards he labours
in his South London garden
on the names of roses

Poetry can draw on many places, meanings and rhymes; it can be clothed in a myriad of forms, take endlessly different journeys and make much of a small moment in time. In this eclectic presence poetry can be an apt medium of expression in the complex world that the modern day botanic garden inhabits. A primary role of these gardens is to share the diversity of the plant world by providing 'botanical snap-shots' for people to view. How these plants are interpreted depends much on labels, settings, stories and of course the people themselves. In this great age of extinction are we presenting 'nature' or has 'nature' already disappeared? Are we just celebrating what we take to be 'nature' and more importantly is that celebration a collective vision?

In his essay 'Sources of Significance: The Garden in our Time' Marc Trieb comments that the world's people share no common definition of the garden. He goes on to discuss a variety of gardens describing some that ask of the viewer and some that tell the viewer, adding that both are valid ways to make a garden. In these multi-layered relationships between viewer and garden, poetry can create oases, heighten tensions, and stimulate endless questions. By having a poet at Chelsea Physic Garden we have begun to question our past, enjoy particular plants, celebrate sensuality and ponder on the naming and ordering of nature. Through this relationship I hope we will discover a broad common ground, between the practice of poetry and the sciences of horticulture and botany.

THERESA BERGNE

Commissioning poetry in gardens

I started thinking of gardens a couple of years ago working on the Public Art programme at Canary Wharf. The programme encompassed a series of commissions in the public spaces of the development designed to encourage people to look at their surroundings in a new way, challenge their expectations, surprise and entertain. Canary Wharf has a number of squares, fountains, river vistas and one rather pretty garden, and in inviting artists to create work in response to these different sites, I became interested in the idea of artists creating work in response to gardens and the landscape.

Gardens have a variety of functions, meanings and associations. The garden is a place of leisure, pleasure, delight and artistry. It is a peaceful haven within an urban landscape, a flash of colour in a sea of grey, a place of meditation, learning, of meeting and nostalgia. The garden represents constancy but is always changing. It is an everyday place, part of our common landscape touched and formed by human hands. It is an active as well as a personal experience.

In all cases however a garden, much like an artists work, can be seen as an expression of an idea within a specific place, dependent on action. Gardening has also become a national pastime – a form of personal expression and individual creativity in a world where opportunity for creativity and expression is increasingly limited and a form of expression which anyone can participate in. It can be a collective and cultural activity, it can strengthen our sense of the world around us and our role within it.

It is with these thoughts in mind that I resolved to commission a number of artists to make work in response to the garden. Wiltshire is the home of many varied gardens. It is also home to an annual festival in Salisbury, known for its clever mix of classical and contemporary work, and a visionary director with whom I share an interest in presenting the arts outside of their usual context and in the public arena. Helen Marriage took me on a trip of the most loved gardens of the local area, and armed me with a list of individuals who had particularly beautiful private gardens which I began visiting.

With time I narrowed down a selection of locations within which I wanted to work. They represented a range of different scale of garden – a hidden chalk valley which had never been ploughed and consequently had 84 different species of wild flowers: God's own garden perhaps; the landscape park of Wilton House; the lesser known allotment gardens of the city of Salisbury; and the beautiful and very personal garden of Heale House.

I decided to work with a number of artists from a range of different artforms, and poetry was an important member of the group. There is of course a classical relationship between poetry and nature, and it seemed appropriate that I should commission a writer to respond to one of the gardens. I had come across a poem by Alice Oswald in *Poetry Review*, 'Song of a Stone', which had captured my imagination, and I set off to buy a copy of her collection of poems *The Thing in the Gap-Stone Stile*. Alice originally trained as a gardener and she has worked at Wisley, for the National Trust, and at Chelsea Physic Garden. I liked the idea of working with someone who had a physical knowledge of gardening who understood and appreciated the labour involved as well as the process.

Heale Garden is a beautiful and special place. It is attached to a house first built in the 16th century, adapted and changed over the years. Charles II sheltered there after the battle of Worcester in 1651. It lies in the Woodford valley, close to the River Avon, and is surrounded by a series of canals which are used to flood the neighbouring fields, and are channelled off into streams to form part of the Japanese water garden. The garden was originally laid out by Harold Peto in 1910 but most of its current character is the result of one woman's work: Lady Anne Rasch.

Lady Anne first started working on the garden in the 1950s. The Japanese garden was a whim of Lady Anne's great great uncle who, after a session as a diplomat in Tokyo, became a strong devotee of Japanese culture, and brought back a magnificent tea-house, huge stone temple lantern and a number of other smaller snow lanterns. This, together with a varied collection of plants, shrubs, musk and other roses, growing in a number of formal settings including an apple tunnel, terraces, and a pergola are arranged in such a way as you 'might arrange cushions on a sofa. The sofa in this case being a garden' as Lady Anne herself described it.

Initially I contacted Alice Oswald and asked if she might like to become involved in the project. She visited the garden on a trip to see some friends in a neighbouring county and agreed. The gardens are open to the public and there is a small and slightly eccentric garden centre attached. Lady Anne's son, and his young wife live in the house, and they responded to my proposal to commission an artist to create something in their garden with cautious enthusiasm. 'As long as they don't leave a large pink blob on the lawn, they're very welcome' was Guy Rasch's response. The ethereal nature of a series of poems, was a little less interventionist than they expected, but a safer option.

On hearing about the Poetry Society's Poetry Places scheme I met with Sarah Maguire and Dawn Sanders of Chelsea Physic Garden and was impressed with their own plans for combining Sarah's writing with a more long term project with local Moroccan women. My own conversations with the Poetry Society started off with equally ambitious plans but it soon became dear that the longer-term residencies had already been allocated, although we would be eligible for a smaller Poetry Places scheme. In any event, both Alice and I were clear that any intervention in the garden itself would need to be carefully thought through, should not be gimmicky, and remain true to the nature of the poems once written.

In November last year, Alice and her family came to spend a week at Heale. Alice spent her days working with the gardener, Gwyn Perry, and meeting the water keeper. In February, just before she had her second child, I went to visit her and collected the poems. It was enormously exciting and we spent some time thinking through how we would put them back into the garden that had inspired them.

We decided in the end to publish a small booklet with all the poems, and a description of how each connected to the garden. We managed to produce a slim volume using local printers and these were put on sale at the garden centre. At the same time we decided to make a sound installation for the period of the festival, with one of the longer poems, 'A Noh Ballad'. Taking its inspiration from the Japanese garden, it is based on a Japanese story about the aerial spirit of the kingfisher. The ballad is a kind of fairy tale and I liked the idea that it should be whispered to you from the depths of a well. The well sits in one of the fields opposite the house, and it was my intention that as you listened to the poem, you could look back across the river at the gardens. A line from another poem, 'The River', was carved in stone by the local masons of Salisbury Cathedral and placed into one of the streams, by the boating pier: 'carries the moon carries the sun but keeps nothing'. The stone is made of a very soft local 'Chicksgrove', which will gradually erode and fade with time.

Alice's poems and the Well elicited a very good response from both audiences attending the Festival's programme and Heale Garden's own garden visitors. All appreciated the fact that little had been done 'to the garden' itself. The poems give cause for reflection, offer a new dimension to the space, and add a new perspective to the garden. They also continue to be sold from the garden shop.

ALICE OSWALD

The Universe in time of rain makes the world alive with noise

1. SOUND

Fixed in one place, normally bent over, staring at the ground for weeds, when you're gardening you rely on your hearing to round out where you are. You become very good at, for example, feeling how much cloud there is by the way a plane-engine echoes; or telling through the pitch of bees the different shapes of flowers.

People often ask me what I like best about gardening. Is it the herbaceous or the alpine or the acid-loving or monocotyledonous aspects that appeal to you? The truth is, it's the sound. I don't know anything lovelier than those free shocks of sound happening against the backsound of your heartbeat. Machinery, spade-scrapes, birdsong, gravel, rain on polythene, macks moving, aeroplanes, seeds kept in paper, potatoes coming out of boxes, high small leaves or large head-height leaves being shaken, frost on grass, strimmers, hoses... also, when you look up, (and your eyes are still half in your ears) the modulation of outlines, the landscape as a physical score, the periodicity of things – weather, daylight, woods, all long unstable rhythms and dissonance. When I'm writing a poem, the first thing I hear is its shape somewhere among all that noise.

I try to avoid conventional metre in favour of this metre that is already actual. I try to keep listening, letting each line grow slowly out of the landscape. I have my left hand cupped like an ear and it feels as if I'm holding my mind in my right hand and a garden in my left. And I can hear two ranges – the range of real sound out of which the poem's melody emerges; and further down, where hearing joins forces with speaking, I can hear sentences, distinct grammatical waves coming off things like waves of energy.

(water – a movement continually bringing itself to light, throwing thought off its surface, a verb clustered with conjunctions...

imagine naming a river every three seconds according to what lies at hand: Water-And-Sewage-Humming-Into-Darkness-Among-Mullet-Under-The-Bent-Body-Of-An-Echo...

my poems are nothing more than a series of extended names spoken together; a kind of complex onomatopoeia, *or 'naming through listening'...)*

It doesn't matter how a poem is made. What's important is that listening, and gardening as a form of listening, is a way of forcing a poem open to what lies bodily beyond it. Because the eye is an instrument tuned to surfaces, but the ear tells you about volume, depth, content – like tapping a large iron shape to find if it's full or not. The ear hears into, not just at what surrounds it. And the whole challenge of poetry is to keep language open, so that what we don't yet know can pass through it.

2. GOLD

Midas, king of Phrygia, was allowed to make a wish. He wished everything he touched would turn to gold. He ran out excited, he touched an oak twig, it went gold; a flint, a clod of earth, an apple – they all deadened into gold. It happened like a failure of the senses, the detail of his surroundings went blurred, slowly took on the coldness and one colour of his mind.

This gold world – dead still, no smell, nothing surprising – is a solipsism, a mind staring at itself. It is Power's flaw and the Writer, King of Paper, often deliberately succumbs to it. Think of pastoral poetry, in which the physical landscape stands for the psychological:

You naked trees, whose shady leaves are lost,

Wherein the byrds were wont to build their bowre,

And now are clothd with mosse and hoary frost,

Instede of bloosmes, where with your buds did flowre;

I see your teares that from your boughes doe raine,

Whose drops in drery ysicles remaine.

Allso my lustfull leafe is dry and sere,

My timely buds with wayling all are wasted;

The blossome which my braunche of youth did beare

With breathed sighes is blowne away and blasted;

And from mine eyes the drizling teares descend,

As on your boughes the ysicles depend.

('The Shephearde's Calendar', Edmund Spenser)

I've always loved poems which express the continuity of man with Nature. But when I started gardening, what enthralled me was the contrariness of Nature – the earth fighting back, refusing to loosen, roots clinging in, cold disabling my fingers. And the weather – as if Midas should feel rain...

After the gales of January 1990, I was sawing up a birch tree. Its bark was coming off in curls of gold, its topmost twigs were on a level with my eyes, and I noticed its unhomelike look (because from a distance, trees look like human excitement, but from close up, they look like nothing at all), and then I began to notice this unhomelike look in other things – the unthroatlike throats of flowers and the no-eyed mud – and it was like a third mind opening, a mind for detail, for thickness, uncanniness, variability – in all places something infinitely distant from myself. I began to want to read poems that could offer an equivalent grace – an encounter with something wholly other.

Hughes said of his writing: 'maybe my concern has been to capture not animals particularly and not poems, but simply things which have a vivid life of their own outside mine'. He had a way of fixing the eyes of things – 'a widening deepening greenness', 'the round angelic eye', 'a black doorway, the eye's pupil' and the energy of his voice is all to do with this pinpoint through which something bigger than the verse pushes in from outside. A style bent by reality: 'these improvised verses are nothing more than this: my own way of getting reasonably close to what is going on, and staying close, and of excluding everything else that might be pressing to interfere with the watching eye. In a sense, the method excludes the poetic process as well...'

3. WORK

'Nature is a world pervaded by externality, in which all things are outside each other in space and time'. I can't remember who said this, but it's a good footnote to that misleading expression a 'nature poet'. If the phrase must be used, then a nature poet is someone concerned with things being outside each other. How should extrinsic forms, man and earth for example, come into contact?

Poirier, addressing this problem in Frost's poetry, writes: 'manual labour in Frost is often an image of the effort to penetrate matter. Such penetration is the precondition for the discovery of an intermediate realm where something in the self and something in things can meet in a system of approximations'.

It's certainly true that when you're digging you become bodily implicated in the ground's world, thought and earth continually passing through each other. You smell it, you feel its strength under your boot, you move alongside it for maybe eight hours and your spade's language (it speaks in short lines of trochees and dactyls: sscrunch turn slot slot, sscrunch turn slot slot) creeps and changes at the same pace as the soil. You can't help being critical of any account of mud that is based on mere glimpsing.

This is not to say that gardeners know the only meaning of mud, but that meaning is something 'working' and provisional, it needs to be picked up and put down and then picked up again over a period of time, according to what needs doing, like any hoe or hand tool. To quote Heidegger (because his name's appropriate): 'the less we just stare at the hammer-thing and the more we seize hold of it and use it, the more primordial does our relation to it become and the more unveiledly is it encountered as that which it is...'.

I was once told, by someone who had seized hold of a spade-thing, that dirt is what you get on tools, mud is what you get on boots, soil is what you grow things in and ground is what you lean on your hoe on. Every job has its dialect. Salmon fishers talk of the 'voler', the unique clean line a salmon makes through water. Most of us don't see the line because we don't know the word.

One way of expressing this attitude to meaning, that it always operates within a work-world, is to suggest, through the notation of poetry, a series of separated frames – something like Emerson's circles: 'the natural world may be conceived as a system of concentric circles, and we now and then detect in Nature slight dislocations, which apprise us that this surface on which we now stand is not fixed, but sliding'. A form establishing and breaking itself as it goes. For this reason, I build poems out of discrete blocks of sound and grammar with huge gaps in between them. But it's not always clear to readers what I'm doing.

As a way of solving the notation problem, I came up with the idea of a mobile poem, in which verses would float free of any particular order: a variable assembly of fixed phrases. This would ensure that the gaps between verses were not just run together and the temptation to read without sound, headlong down a page to find the meaning, would be thwarted. You might call it a 'working' poem, in the sense that you can see the movement going on between groups of words.

4. THE HEALE PROJECT

Last autumn, I was asked by Theresa Bergne to contribute to her Secret Gardens project, for the Salisbury Festival. The remit was to write five or six poems inspired by Heale Gardens. These would be the basis for a number of installations by different artists, to be shown in the garden over the festival period.

I took on the commission because I wanted to have a real mobile poem made, probably out of metal; to hang it from a tree, where the wind would keep chiming it. I was also intrigued by the idea of putting texts back into the landscape. I've been thinking about language as a physical object for 10 years now ever since visiting Iain Hamilton Finlay's garden at Stonypath, in Scotland.

His poems appear as puns, quotes, emblems, proverbs, fragments worked into the landscape. They're normally very short – about one line – which gives them the virtue of inscriptions, that all their words exist simultaneously.

In a literary text, words melt away as you read them. In a concrete text, they continue to influence each other. The result is something like Barbara Hepworth's Mary-figure sculptures: a composition of separate but connected forms. Ideally, this is how I would like every sentence to sound. 'I heard twa corbies making

and underfoot and in the heart and

keeping that promise upon which the sunlight takes its bearings

like through each leaf light is being somehow
put together in a rush and wedged in a narrow place

SONNET

towards winter flowers, forms of ecstatic water,
    chalk lies dry with all its throat open.
winter flowers last maybe one frost
    chalk drifts its heap through billions of slow sea-years
    rain and pools and opens its wombs,
    bows its back, shows its bone.
    both closing towards each other
    at the dead end of the year – one
    woken through, the others thrown into flower,
holding their wings at the ready in an increasing state of crisis.
                burrowed into and crumbled, carrying
these small supernumerary powers founded on breath:
    chalk with all its pits and pores,
winter flowers, smelling of a sudden entering elsewhere

IDEOGRAM FOR GREEN

For the Chinese Garden. I conceived it as a mobile poem, in which verses would float free of any particular order but this was not, in the end, practicable. It should read down the page, like an ordinary poem, but with the feeling that all its phrases are simultaneous. Like an ideogram. I was interested in Fenollosa's claim that Chinese ideograms are pictures of all the associations that compile a word. So this is an accumulation of instances, a heap of different conditions-for-green...

SONNET

For the vegetable garden. The landscape at Heale is chalk. This poem is about the difference between chalk and flower, in particular the smell of those flowers that were out in late November: Wintersweet, Viburnum bodnantense, a green rose... I chose sonnet form because a sonnet can reconcile a tension. This poem has five beats to a line, like a conventional sonnet, but any amount of syllables. But instead of rhyming, it uses the Hebrew verse-form of matching and reversing pairs of ideas, (like a psalm). Rhyme would have given chalk and flower something in common. This scheme sort of twists them round each other without fusing them.

1

2

Papaver: Poppy
'Poppies in October'   by Sylvia Plath

Even the sun-clouds this morning
    cannot manage such skirts.
Nor the woman in the ambulance
Whose red heart blooms through
    her coat so astoundingly—

From *Collected Poems* (London: Faber & Faber, 1965)
© Sylvia Plath, 1965; renewed by Ted Hughes

7

BIOGRAPHIES

Theresa Bergne is an independent curator and producer, who commissions artists to create work for a variety of urban and rural locations including gardens in Greenwich and Wiltshire and the public spaces of Canary Wharf.

Eleanor Cooke has published three collections of poetry: *A Kind of Memory*, *Who Killed Prees Heath?* and *Secret Files*. She is an experienced lecturer and broadcaster and has written several plays.

Gerry Loose is a poet, the Managing Editor for Survivors' Poetry Scotland and a lifelong gardener. His publications include *Tongues of Stone: a measure*, *The Elementary Particles* and *The Holistic Handbook for Scotland*.

Sarah Maguire has published two collections: *Spilt Milk* and *The Invisible Mender*, which was a Poetry Book Society Special Commendation. A trained horticulturist, she worked as a gardener before becoming a full-time writer and broadcaster.

Alice Oswald's first collection, *The Thing in the Gap-Stone Stile* was a Poetry Book Society Choice and shortlisted for the T S Eliot Prize. Inspired by Homer, she trained as a gardener and has worked at Chelsea Physic Garden and Tapley Park, Devon.

Dawn Sanders is Head of Education at Chelsea Physic Garden.

Photographs

Front cover: Sarah Maguire at Chelsea Physic Garden. Credit: Gina Glover

1. School visit to Birmingham Botanical Gardens. Credit: Bill Graham

2. Eleanor Cooke at Birmingham Botanical Gardens. Credit: Bill Graham

3. The rock garden at Birmingham Botanical Gardens. Credit: Bill Graham

4. Theresa Bergne at Alice Oswald's whispering well in Heale Garden. Credit: Steve Day

5. Poetry in the stream at Heale Garden. Credit: Steve Day

6. Sarah Maguire and Dawn Sanders in Chelsea Physic Garden. Credit: Gina Glover

7. Poetry at Chelsea Physic Garden. Credit: Gina Glover

ELEANOR COOKE

Leading them down
the garden path

The ladies from the BBC arrived in time for lunch. One carried a clipboard, the other wore glasses. They were both hungry. It was raining –

a sea of branches casting green light

– so they decided to eat first and look round the garden afterwards.

The clip-board explained that the feature would be about writers and their gardens, adding that they had visited some 'very grand' gardens in the last few days. The glasses said quietly to no one in particular that the cottage was a funny little place.

It was: tiny, trapped in a half-circle of high sandstone cliffs, it squatted like an old crone relieving herself under the trees which surrounded it. The garden had been laid out by Maggie, my husband's previous wife. We had spent two days hauling out weeds, cutting and trimming and generally tidying up, in the hope that something of the enchantment Maggie had planted would touch the visitors.

After lunch we went outside. 'Where', the clip-board asked, adjusting her borrowed umbrella while we stood growing damper by the minute, 'do you sit and get inspiration?'.

I explained that I didn't: I used the garden to dig and to work off the frustrations of the recalcitrant muse.

I wasn't surprised to hear next day, by telephone, that the BBC had decided not to film the garden, or interview me about the role of the garden in my creative life.

It is ironic that this, of all the gardens I have tended, should be the one to attract the interest of the media. In almost any other of the places I have lived, I would have been able to satisfy their not unreasonable expectations of a poet's garden: I could have regaled them with stories of ancient apple trees – shown them ridges and furrows like waves of the sea across the lawn, where milkmaids grew in their hundreds in May. And gifts – Michaelmas daisies in fountains of pale purple, and phlox, a present from the gardener at a rather grand estate (they'd have liked that) where more than twenty different colours bloomed in a huge bed. Inspiration! I could have told them about inspiration. But I didn't. The garden they came to see wasn't my garden: it was nothing to do with me.

Most of us can remember our first garden. I was five when my father marked out my first plot. I waited in an agony of suspense for the lupins I'd planted to come up, and when they did – spavin specimens of bifurcate minimalism – my father dug the plot over, understandably blind to the small miracle he was burying alive. A boy I knew suffered a worse trauma: he decided to create his own compost heap, a heaving mass of rotting vegetation which his enraged parents bagged up and took to the local tip. (He grew up to be a professor of philosophy – a nihilist with an obsessive interest in Gilles de Rais.)

I think it's over-rated, giving children a garden: it's a much better idea to take them to a garden where there are no demands made on them, and no expectations. The park will do; or their school garden. I was working with a group of primary school children in their school playing field, when one of them discovered that, with an ear against the trunk of a cherry tree, he could hear the tree talking.

The tree words slide out of the trunk like a tapping shadow.

A piece of unlooked-for magic.

Public gardens don't belong to us (except in a self-consciously civic sense); nor is it incumbent on us to make our mark on them, tend them, or nurture them. They exist only to give themselves to us in moments of wonder: like the moment when I came out of a dark tunnel into the hidden Chinese Garden at Biddulph, before the restoration work had begun. How can one respond to such a moment – by falling on one's knees, singing, weeping, making love there and then with whoever it is you happen to be standing next to? I suspect that none of these options is listed in the guidelines to National Trust officials, let alone recommendations of how to deal with such excesses! But poetry – yes.

Poetry lies in wait for moments like these.

If you can take children to a Botanical Garden, the magic is almost guaranteed. The Botanical Garden in Birmingham is one such place, an out-of-time experience, the horticultural equivalent of walking on the moon. The Poetry Society's Poetry Places scheme offered me the chance to work there with school-children and their teachers in the autumn of 1998. The children were of different ages and abilities: one group was from a school for children with severe learning difficulties, another comprised young people from the top stream of a comprehensive school; the third was from an outer ring primary school, the fourth from an inner ring primary with a high proportion of children with English as their second language.

The days started with riddles: teachers on their induction day had written their own to add to the ones I created to start them off, and these formed the nucleus of the trails.

Heavenly music?
Listen, don't finger.
I may heal, or make you sick
if you dare to linger.
(Angel's Trumpet)

The children chased round, searching for the answers, and then created new ones.

I have leaves you can surf on, on the waves of the wind.

(Banana Tree)

Tell me what you want, what you really really want. You want a clue?

My little fat toes wriggle in the mud.

(Ginger)

My leaves are like dragons dreaming of blood.

(Pelargonium)

The riddles paved the way for imagery. Soon, the canopy of leaves in the Tropical House outlined

jigsaw pieces of blue which puzzle the sky

the fish in the pool were

bright stars, gold and silver in the deep end;

foliage fastened itself in someone's imagination as

the waving of hair-like stems in the distance

and the leaves became

witches brooms ripping the moonlit sky,

sounding the adventures of a thousand wild nights.

When the children were asked to describe a plant for a blind person, fruits became

light glowing on the tree,

leaves were

warm rain trickling from a bright sky,

seed pods

an army of knots on the bark.

The kids were high on poetry, and so were their teachers:

dappled light paints and puckers
like the skin of old apples.

I began to suspect that it was the plants who were re-inventing us, not we who were re-inventing them.

I asked them to imagine the spirit of the plants, telling them tales from Ancient Greece and the Punjab about ghosts trapped in trees, to lick the muse into shape. A procession of stories followed – rebellious daughters trapped, forever weeping dragons; murderers whose eyes follow every movement from their green eyrie – watchful, plotting.

Was it the gardens who performed the magic, or the children, or me? I did my homework of course – it's what I do, what I'm paid to do. But before I spoke a word, before I told a story, or initiated a cunning artifice, poetry had us by the throat.

The place let poetry in. As the children entered the glasshouses, you could hear the gasp, feel the twist in the gut: one of the teachers said, 'I can put a tick in the "awe-and-wonder" box'.

In the entrance hall of the gardens, there are aviaries full of budgerigars and parakeets. Their voices fill the space, and, as you enter the Tropical House and the doors close behind you, recordings of the sounds of the rain forest are piped over the sound of water filling and re-filling the pool. One of the boys from the school for children with severe learning difficulties said very little – he volunteered two or three images, one or two words to complete a line. But he sang all day, in a perfect imitation of the caged birds. His teacher tried to stop him, but the birdsong kept escaping.

Visiting the garden gave us all the chance to touch another world and let it touch us. We held on to the experience in whatever way we could. Glen did it by singing: the rest of us did it the only way poets can. With words.

Speak to the sepal nations

Dianthus barbatus; Lunaria annua; Physostegia virginina; Solidago canadensis; Lychnis flos-jovis; Kniphofia uvaria; Aster farreri.

At a very early age, my grandmother gave me a little patch of garden in which I grew nothing but mint – very carefully tended; about that time I first read in the *Junior Weekend Book* (at a time when childhood was all weekend)

> *there was a man of double deed*
> *who sowed his garden full of seed*

and at that time words and plants came together for me, shaping my outlook and perspective. My working life has been in both fields.

Imagine then, my excitement at being let loose in a Botanic Garden and being asked, in effect, to bring plants and poetry together in the public eye.

Glasgow's Botanic Gardens is unique among gardens I've visited in that it appears to belong to the people of Glasgow. On any day when there is sun, the whole Garden resembles a beach in summer – picnickers, sunbathers, illicit ball-players, newspaper readers, students and dog-walkers covering every inch of grass and all the benches.

Any other day in the early morning will see elderly Chinese women and men, gently practicing Tai-chi and Chigong; as the day progresses, schoolkids and parents hurry through, the salwar kamiz more plentiful than the kilt; Scots, English, Urdu and Cantonese vowels and consonants apriling from lips and landing in the flower beds and on the grass.

Glasgow also has a thriving and healthy culture of writing and literature, priding itself on its mastery of at least three languages: Gaelic, Scots and English. Writers' groups abound throughout the city; interest in poetry is very high. On the way to the station a while back I had a long conversation with my taxi driver about the poetry of an eminent Scottish poet. That the driver had been reading the work in a language he was not born to is the remarkable fact of our conversation. In Glasgow, I've been to readings in many languages including Urdu *mashairas* based loosely on the Persian *ghazal*. This sense of linguistic and cultural diversity is what I hoped to bring to the fore during my residency.

Cultural diversity. A phrase which also applies to gardening, and reflects my own attitude to gardens (of all kinds – I've been a gardener of flowerbeds as well as a market gardener and farmer at various times) – monoculture is as bad for the soul as it is for the soil. I quickly decided that there should be no writers' workshops, but could apply the strengths of the Gardens and the people who used them, together with the human delight in tradition and spectacle to fulfil my residency remit.

Gardeners love names and naming. Taxonomy also is at the heart of a Botanic Garden. The names I list above are of common border plants which have arrived here during the past four centuries, and have delighted gardeners who have given them names which are metaphoric in themselves – Sweet William, Honesty, Obedient plant, Goldenrod, Flower of Jove, Red Hot Poker. Other plants, in the economic section of the main range of hot houses here, offer up variations of names from the languages of people who first knew them – *Coffea arabica, Carica papaya, Thebroma cacao, Pogostemon patchouly* – after Linnaeus had classified them.

Themes were emerging. Diversity of languages spoken and written in Glasgow (with, as an example, more Urdu speakers than Gaelic speakers) including the babble of tongues on the Garden's identification labels. Many people using the Gardens would know the plants by names other than the Scientific binomial classifying name, or its English common name. (A nice irony that plant hunters' trophies were on view to people who look to other parts of the world as their original homeland – plants, people and language in post-colonial reunion.) It's a small step from there to the certain knowledge that plant and garden references exist in the poetic traditions of the languages now commonly spoken in Glasgow (other than English, Scots and Gaelic – the three leids).

Add to this the feeling of public ownership of the Botanics, as everyone calls them, and the thronging of the Garden on any excuse at any time.

Events, then, had to be the order of the day – including spectacle and tradition as well as a strong participatory strand at a language level. I devised two major events building on existing traditions – the cloutie tree and the May Day Parade.

Just so that the message of plants and poetry coming together would escape no-one using the park, there would also be a series of readings by poets with a foot in the gardening camp, performances, book launches and school events using the Botanics' natural resources. A parallel series of interventions would ensure that this presence would be maintained by selecting poems from Scottish resident poets to sit alongside the plants to which they refer throughout the Gardens. These latter (some 30 to date) have ranged from a poem in Gaelic about foxgloves to poems about specific trees, Lithops divergens, pitcher plants; in

English, Chinese and Urdu; scattered throughout the gardens as the plants emerge or as poems are given – this, another theme – to involve other poets in the project.

A quick run through the events and happenings during my residency so far (the initial six months Poetry Places residency was extended by Glasgow City Council) demonstrates the enthusiasm which I have met. Curators, managers, gardeners, rangers, schoolteachers, poets, children; anybody I've talked to (and sometimes it feels like everyone in Glasgow) has offered help, expertise, given their time and, in some cases, money to the residency ideas. The latter is important, since without financial support for events from Glasgow City Council and one or two businesses (for specific details) there would have been a limited range of possibilities open to me.

Apart from the two big events, there have been five readings (two with musicians) in the Gardens, involving thirteen well known poets; book launches; workshops by visiting writers; a book launch with associated exhibition of plant photographs and poems, a Halloween performance of poems and drama by students from the Royal Scottish Academy of Music and Drama – poems everywhere, including the fishpond; work with schoolchildren which ended with the massed floating down the river Kelvin (running through the gardens) of hundreds of paper boats, each with the cargo of a poem about water written by a school pupil; and, despite my 'no-workshops' rule, a set of workshops (with young mothers in drug rehabilitation) to do with food and the food plants of the Gardens, which produced remarkable poems and poetic recipes. (A theme which is continuing with the help of two local vegetarian restaurants, one Indian, one European; including menus [and recipes] based around the possibilities of poetry in the names of threatened vegetable varieties which will be grown and eaten by restaurant customers at a harvest feast. One section of one menu reads – Mushroom Cloud Hash: Silsden Bomb red cabbage, Giant Improved Flak carrot, Brown Soldier bean, De'Ath's bean, Black Jet soya bean.)

There was also a public 'DancePerformancePoetry' event in December in a biting wind, during which one person informed me that the flower-clad performers were suffering from frost bite – she wanted to call an ambulance, such was her involvement and concern – and which stopped the traffic by the Garden's main gate. We also celebrated the 80th birthday of Scotland's poet laureate, Edwin Morgan, open to all, with sax player Tommy Smith and readers Tom Leonard, Ron Butlin and Liz Lochhead (and a fine cake – though sadly there was no time to make poetic cake recipes or menus). I mention all this in a rather breathless hurry-fashion to show how the right idea in the right place at the right time can take off – as this residency undoubtedly has, involving hundreds of people in a hot-house of cultural and linguistic celebration of poetry and plants.

> *she is the white wave blown by the wind*
> *she is the wind that blows the white wave*

was written on one of the ribbons that was returned to me to be hung in the Botanics' Valentine Tree.

The Valentine tree built on two very simple traditions – the exchange of poems of love on St Valentine's Day, and the Scottish tradition of the 'cloutie tree', where rags (cloths, clouts), poems, prayers and tokens are hung in a tree, usually associated with a healing well. It helped that St Valentine's remains rest in a Franciscan church in the city. Members of the public, as well as poets and other writers, were invited to write a poem of love and hang it in a large beech tree in the Botanic Gardens on St Valentine's Day. Poems could be on any aspect of love, as well as addressed to a lover, and could be sent for hanging by me if the writer could not be there for the event. With the invitation, a red ribbon was sent for poems to be written on. (The ribbons were provided by a local textile company as in-kind sponsorship – I'm keen on getting everyone in on the act.)

I suspected that this would prove a popular way of both encouraging the writing of poetry and bringing people into the

Gardens. I only realised the scale of interest when people began phoning the Gardens requesting ribbons for friends and lovers – the ribbons ran out in the first couple of days (300 metres of ribbon), and I began to comprehend the task I had to hang them all. It took me a long morning up a ladder in biting wind and hail (Scotland in February).

On Valentine's Day a couple of hundred people turned up with poems to tie into the tree – poems on paper, cloth, ribbons, embroidered, on card and laminated, photomontage poems. Poems in Gaelic, Scots, Urdu, Bengali, Chinese, Greek, Polish, German, Sanskrit and Tibetan and English were all hung during a lull in the sleet. In the semi-tropical Kibble Palace nearby was Gar Ming Hui, a Chinese paper artist demonstrating the folding of winged hearts. Many folk made their own, wrote a spontaneous poem, went outside and hung it in the Valentine tree.

After the tree event was a reading attended (a weekday lunchtime) by more than a hundred people. Burns love poems were read together with her own poems (in the Doric) by Sheena Blackhall; Kathleen Jamie read poems in Scots and English, interspersed by the music from two fiddles ringing round the central glazed dome that forms the main part of the curvilinear glass Kibble Palace at the heart of the Botanic Gardens.

Wordwort – Verbum speciosum *'a highly variable perennial. It is propagated chiefly by means of "books", which contain its thin, papery leaves. It is fertilized by the human imagination. A bed of wordwort is called a "poem". It has many uses, for healing, soothing, as a tonic, and in combination with other plants, such as the Songwort (Cantus mellifluous)'.*

This definition, supplied by the poet and botanist Colin Will of the Royal Botanic Gardens, Edinburgh, sums up my approach to the Glasgow Botanic Gardens Residency.

In one apt definition, of a plant of my imagination, its tone sets the playful and inclusive notions I have for a successful residency. Play is a very serious business redolent with poetic opportunity. It also clearly transcends borders, seeding everywhere. If it can transcend the traditional Edinburgh / Glasgow rivalry it can go anywhere.

For our May Day celebration, people at large were invited to submit a single favourite word each. These words would then be made into individual banners or word flags and hung all around the gardens on May Day. Inspiration for the event was drawn from both the wild plants of the Botanic Gardens (weeds) – figwort, toothwort etc – and the May Day rallies and workers' celebrations (with banners) held until recently in the city. If people could not be there on May Day, they had the option of sending me their words as flags or as words I would turn into banners. I was surprised at the number and variety of words, which were sent in all the languages of Scotland (including one poet's favourite word from the Latin of *Duns Scotus*).

At the same time as walking round hanging words and reading others' words, people were invited to make poems from the words as they wandered the Gardens.

At noon on May Day, we flew the Poetry Flag (the whole event was called Flying the Flag for Poetry) which had been specially made for the event by banner and textile artist Pam Sandals. The flag is 3 metres by 5 fi metres. It is divided in two by a curving diagonal line, yellow and blue. On one side, blue on yellow is sewn 'word'; on the other, yellow on blue is 'wort'. Yellow is for *Iris pseudacoras*, whose common name is the yellow flag, long associated with poets ('yellow flag flowers blowing in the wind' – Gerard Manley Hopkins in his journal for 1873). Blue since the herbalist John Gerard in 1597 said 'it doth in two daies at the most take away the blewenesse' – a little pun there on the blues and the smiles I hoped to raise. Gerard also called it the *'floure-de-Loose'* with a little creative mis-spelling. I like that. Word for poetry and wort, the old but still current name for a plant. Wordwort the flag to be flown at any event of poetry at the Gardens in the future. The flag was hoisted up the 60-foot flagpole to the music of the pipes and the cheers and clapping of gathered people, poets and banner-makers.

After pinning up more poem-word-flags from trees, everyone went to the reading which followed in the Kibble Palace, with Tom Leonard and Chris Dolan. The heat, for the first time in the year was intense. To their credit the audience, of about a hundred, good-humouredly sweltered to the words of the poets.

Throughout the residency I've interpreted poetry very broadly. My aims have been to celebrate diversity both of poetry and plants, not imposing my own views, but by providing a framework within which people could operate – make poetry and take a fresh look at the plants of the Botanic Gardens. Like a gardener, I planted some seeds, and in due course watched them germinate; thinning out some and encouraging others. I've watched some hybridize and others fail. From the beginning I've been keen to involve and listen to everyone – Garden Curators, other poets and the public as well as visual artists and lens based artists. I've had every possible help from all the staff at the Botanics – making an enjoyable residency one to relish.

There remain seeds which have still to germinate, like the concrete poetry and sculpture collaboration, or the Renga platform, complete with poets, to tour Botanic Gardens throughout Scotland. Some ideas were impractical, like printing invitations on fallen leaves. Some little squibs will remain – like the Botanic labels with scientific and common names (identical to all others in the gardens) for plants such as dandelions, daisies, Japanese knotweed and giant Hogweed. I've also commissioned a number of Scottish poets to make a poem about a plant, to be made in the format of a Botanic black label, restricted to that size and hung or planted next to the poem it refers to.

My own poems, though not part of all these activities, have flourished. I have notebooks full and various poems complete, like the Taxonomy series and the Glasgow Botanic Walks series – drawing from plant names. There is also the chance that the residency will become permanent. Then I'll have a chance to work on the four box-files of clippings and ideas I've accumulated, before handing over to another resident poet. I'll also be leaving a lasting legacy in the form of a poem on glass for the soon-to-be refurbished Kibble Palace – a poem reading from the inside against a backdrop of Glasgow sky and a foreground of plants – for visitors to happen upon – the way poetry takes place.

Sepals are parts of the calyx that in the bud stage enclose and protect the other flower parts, usually green or brown, mostly overlooked in the show of the flower. One newspaper described me as the bard for the begonias, poet for the pansies; My title – 'Speak to the sepal nations' (from Barry MacSweeney's 'Ode to the Unborn') is, I think justified. In addition, I would like to think I've spoken a little for the sepal nations.

BIOGRAPHIES

Theresa Bergne...

Eleanor Cooke...

Gerry Loose is a poet, the Managing Editor for Survivors' Poetry Scotland and a lifelong gardener. His publications include *Tongues of Stone*; *a measure*; *The Elementary Particles*; and *The Holistic Handbook for Scotland*.

Sarah Maguire has published two collections, *Spilt Milk* and *The Invisible Mender,* (which was a Poetry Book Society Special Commendation). A trained horticulturist, she worked as a gardener before becoming a full-time writer and broadcaster.

Alice Oswald...

Dawn Sanders...

ACKNOWLEDGMENTS

'Botany' appears by permission of Michael Longley.

Photographs were taken by Gina Glover, Bill Graham and Steve Day.